Writing 6–7

Author: Stephanie Cooper
Illustrators: Emma Holt and Chris McGhie

Letts

How to use this book

Look out for these features!

IN THE ACTIVITIES

The parents' notes at the top of each activity will give you:

- a simple explanation about what your child is learning
- an idea of how you can work with your child on the activity.

This small page number guides you to the back of the book, where you will find further ideas for help.

These magic stars provide useful facts and helpful hints!

AT THE BACK OF THE BOOK

Every activity has a section for parents containing:

- further explanations about what the activity teaches
- games that can be easily recreated at home
- questions to ask your child to encourage their learning
- tips on varying the activity if it seems too easy or too difficult for your child.

You will also find the answers at the back of the book.

HELPING YOUR CHILD AS THEY USE THIS BOOK

Why not try starting at the beginning of the book and work through it? Your child should only attempt one activity at a time. Remember, it is best to learn little and often when we are feeling wide awake!

EQUIPMENT YOUR CHILD WILL NEED

- a pencil for writing
- an eraser for correcting mistakes
- coloured pencils for drawing and colouring in.

You might also like to have ready some spare paper and some collections of objects (for instance, small toys, Lego bricks, buttons...) for some of the activities.

Contents

Past and present tenses **4**
More past and present tenses **6**
Writing instructions **8**
Finish the rhyme **10**
Opposites **12**
One words from two **14**
Alphabetical order **16**
Syllables **18**
Writing questions **20**
Ridiculous rhymes **22**
Make up a rhyme **24**
Famous sayings **26**
Writing a different story **28**
Writing a profile **30**
Nearly the same **32**
Writing rhymes **34**
Writing tongue twisters **36**
Writing riddles **38**
Writing a story **40**
Writing information **42**
Further activities **44**
Celebration! **48**

Past and present tenses

Write these sentences again but put them in the past tense.

walked	**jumped**	**laughed**	**pushed**
	listened	**knocked**	

I am jumping

____

I am walking

____

We are listening

____

I am knocking

____

We are laughing

____

I am pushing

____

Parents 44

- This activity will help your child learn more about writing in the past and present tenses.
- The illustrations will help provide more ideas.

Write these sentences again but put them in the present tense. Don't forget to use **am** or **are**!

cooking planting picking pulling watching playing

We cooked

____

We played

____

I watched

____

We pulled

____

I picked

____

We planted

____

More past and present tenses

Read this story about Raj, Polly and Peter Parrot.

1

Raj leaves the house. He forgets to shut the bird cage.

2

Polly and Peter fly out.

3

They eat all the bird seed.

4

They knock over Mum's flowers.

5

The cat chases after them.

6

They go back into their cage.

This activity will help your child learn to recognise past and present tenses.

Talking about events will help them to hear the difference.

Parents 44

Now help Raj write about what happened.

saw knocked ate flew chased left went

Yesterday I went out. I ______________ the bird cage door open.

Polly and Peter ______________ out.

They ________ all the bird seed, and ______________ over Mum's flowers.

When the cat ______________ them, he ______________ after them.

The parrots ______________ back into their cage.

Writing instructions

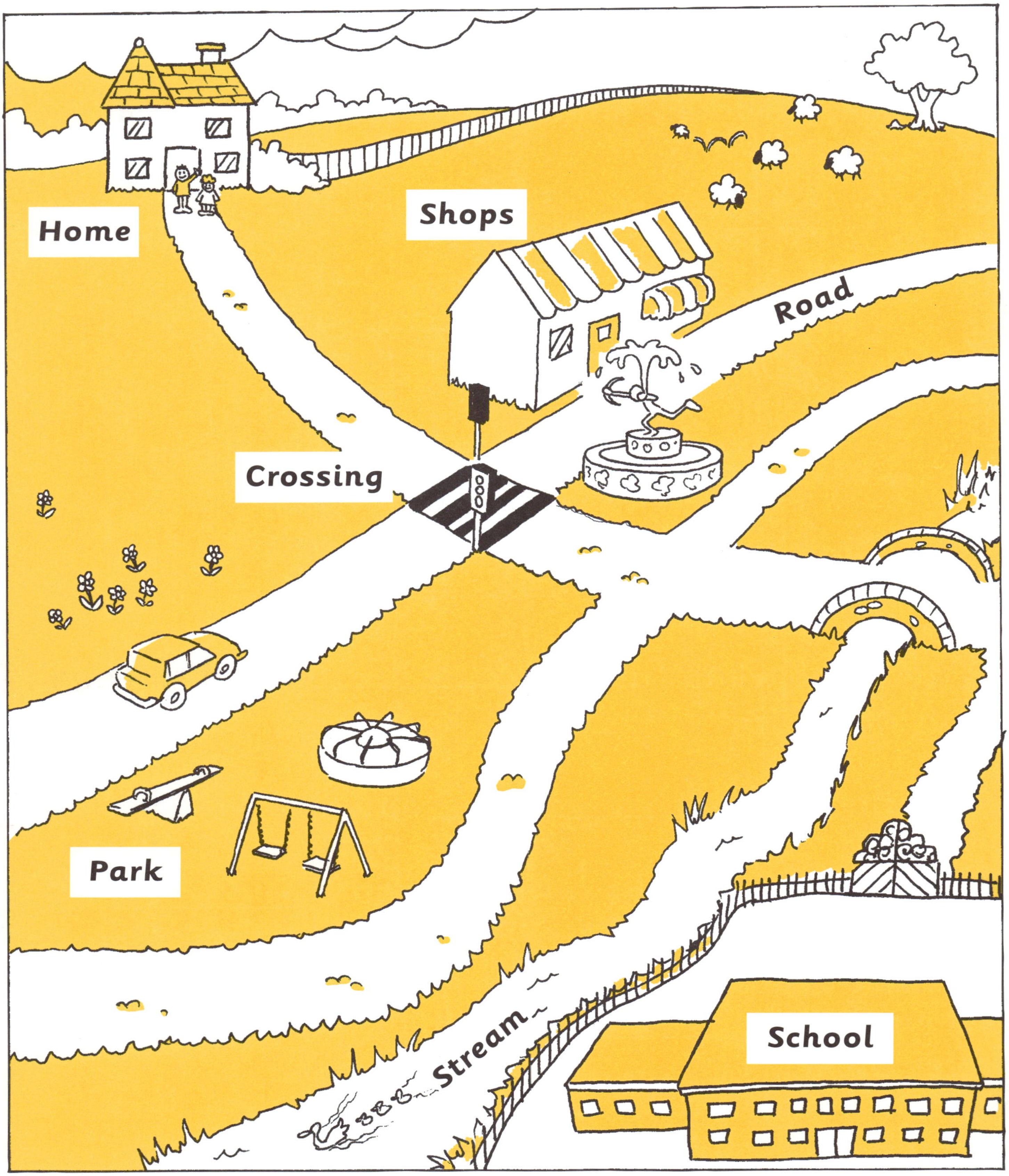

Parents

- This activity will help your child learn how to write simple instructions.
- Ask them to label the map first, to make them think about what Samuel walks past.

44

Samuel is starting a new school.
Write 4 instructions for Samuel and his dad so they know how to get there.

1 ______________________________

____

____

2 ______________________________

____

____

3 ______________________________

____

____

4 ______________________________

____

____

Finish the rhyme

Finish each sentence to make it rhyme.

I met a dog sitting on a ____________.

I met a man jumping on a ____________.

I met a mouse playing in a ____________.

I met a goat chewing up a ____________.

- This activity will enable your child to invent rhyming sentences, using their knowledge of rhyme.
- The rhyming words need to have the same number of syllables to scan.

I met a wizard chatting to a ________.

I met as fish swimming in a ________.

I met a toad hopping on the ________.

road house coat lizard dish log van

Opposites

Fill in the gaps with words that have the opposite meaning.

hot cold

________ push

hard ________

________ smooth

high ________

________ short

fat ________

big ________

________ fast

up ________

________ noisy

Parents

44

- This activity will help your child understand opposites, and the differences in their meaning.
- Help them understand by talking about opposites, like 'smooth' and 'rough', around the home.

Change the underlined words to give each sentence the opposite meaning. You may have to change some other words so they make sense.

1. This drink is boiling hot.

2 This jumper is very rough .

3. That is too high for me to reach.

4. My ruler is too short to measure you.

One word from two

Which two words go together to make each 'answer' word?

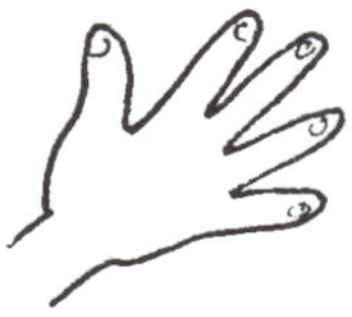  

hand + bag = handbag

__________ + __________ = milkman

__________ + __________ = pancake

__________ + __________ = teaspoon

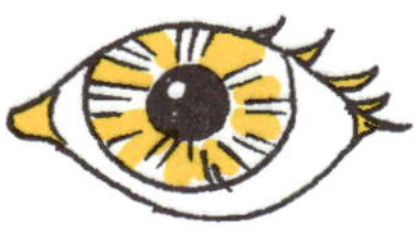  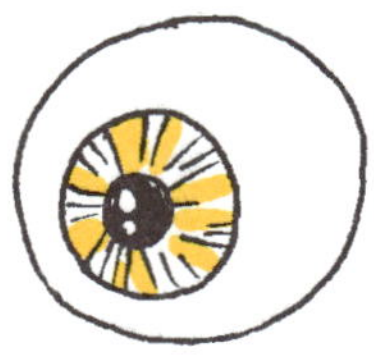

__________ + __________ = eyeball

Parents 45

- This activity shows how a compound word is made by adding two words together.
- To help, ask your child to say each word slowly first.

______ + ______ = snowman

______ + ______ = butterfly

______ + ______ = bookshelf

______ + ______ = ______

______ + ______ = ______

Alphabetical order

Help Mrs Carter sort out these names in her class register. They must be in alphabetical order.

Roxanne Jackson	Michelle Knight
Amy Fisher	Charlie Adams
Kylie Irons	Parmi Dhak
Laura Groves	Sam Evans
Charlotte Hard	Christopher Baker
Nicholas Long	Abena Clarke

Parents

45

- This activity will help your child to place words in alphabetical order.
- Point out that they should use the first letter in each surname.

1 ______________________________

2 ______________________________

3 ______________________________

4 ______________________________

5 ______________________________

6 ______________________________

7 ______________________________

8 ______________________________

9 ______________________________

10 ______________________________

11 ______________________________

12 ______________________________

Z Y X W V

O Q S U

N P R T

Syllables

daffodil =

daff / o / dil = 3 beats

cat = 1 beat

dinosaur =

di / no / saur = ☐ beats

children =

________ / ________ = ☐ beats

dinner =

________ / ________ = ☐ beats

Parents 45

- This activity will help your child to discriminate syllables orally and in writing.
- Make sure they say each word aloud to hear the syllables.

How many beats does each of these words have?
Tick the correct column. The first one has been done for you

	1	2	3
writing		✓	
going			
sister			
people			
bed			
two			
fantastic			
water			
elephant			
what			
mummy			

Writing questions

What? Where? When? Who?
These are all **question words**. Question words go at the beginning of a question.

Parents

45

This activity will enable your child to turn statements into questions, using 'what', 'where', 'when' and 'who'.

Remind them to use question marks.

Jack has been talking to a reporter. Here are his answers to some questions. But what were the questions?

Q. ______________________________

A. My name is Jack.

Q. ______________________________

A. I live with my mum at the bottom of the beanstalk.

Q. ______________________________

A. I planted the magic beans yesterday.

Q. ______________________________

A. First I climbed up the beanstalk. Then I met a giant, and a goose that laid golden eggs.

Q. ______________________________

A. Now I am going to chop down the beanstalk before the giant climbs down!

Ridiculous rhymes

Say this rhyme out loud. Write the number of syllables in each line inside the box.

number of syllables

Doctor Foster went to Gloucester

In a shower of rain.

He stepped in a puddle

Right up to his middle

And never went there again.

This activity will enable your child to use humorous verse as a structure for their own writing.

Remind them which words need to rhyme.

Parents 45

Now try this one.

Mrs Tublin went to Dublin
In a terrible storm.
She started to worry
And hurry and hurry
But didn't get there 'til dawn.

Try to write your own rhyme.
Here are some first lines to help you.

Mr Lithgow went to Glasgow

____

____

____

____

Mrs Farley went to Barnsley

____

____

____

____

Make up a rhyme

Fatima has written some ideas that she wants to use in a poem. Can you help her to write it?

Parents

46

- This activity will help your child write their own poems using jottings and words.
- They don't need to use all the words suggested.

Write your poem here.

Famous sayings

Which story character said these things?
Write the correct name under the words.

1. "I am a good boy," he lied, and his nose grew longer.

   ____

2. "I'll huff and I'll puff and I'll blow your house down."

   ____

3. "Grandma! What big teeth you have!"

   ____

4. "Somebody has been sitting in my chair, and they've broken it!"

   ____

The evil wolf

Little Red Riding Hood

Baby bear

Pinocchio

Parents

46

- This activity will help your child use key words and phrases from traditional stories.
- Encourage your child to be imaginative when story-writing.

Now try to write one story using all 4 characters and all 4 sentences.

Writing a different story

You are going to rewrite a well-known story.

The three little pigs lived together in the same house. One day, they went for a walk in the woods nearby. While they were out, the wolf came knocking at their door.

Parents

- This activity will enable your child to write a different version of a familiar story.
- Remind them about trying the porridge, the chairs and the beds.

46

Use what you know about Goldilocks and the Three Bears to help you write a new story about the three little pigs. What happens when the three pigs come home and they find the wolf asleep upstairs?

Write your story here.

Writing a profile

Write about these fairy story characters. Say what each one looks like, where they live, what they do in their story, and if they are a good or a bad character.

The troll from The 3 Billy Goats Gruff.

The small Billy from The 3 Billy Goats Gruff.

Parents 46

This activity will teach your child how to write character profiles.

Ask plenty of questions, to get your child to write in more detail.

The giant from Jack and the Beanstalk.

Jack from Jack and the Beanstalk.

Nearly the same

Write another word which means the same as these words.

hot ____________________

freezing ____________________

dazzling ____________________

enormous ____________________

quiet ____________________

pretty ____________________

nice ____________________

noisy ____________________

happy ____________________

shiny ____________________

dull ____________________

nasty ____________________

Parents

- This activity will help your child use other words to add variety to writing.
- Make sure they avoid the over-use of words like 'nice'.

46

Think of a different word for the underlined words in these sentences.

1. The light was too bright.

______________________________.

2. The weather was cold.

______________________________.

3. It was a pleasant day.

______________________________.

4. The music was too loud.

______________________________.

Writing rhymes

apple and pears →  → **stairs**

dog and bone →  → **phone**

Bill and Ben →  → **pen**

stop and stare →  → **chair**

roof and floor →  → **door**

finger and thumb →  → **mum**

Parents

- This activity will help your child to write their own sentences using rhyme.
- Point out that some rhymes sound the same, but are spelled differently, such as 'stare' and 'chair'.

47

This is what happened to Rory Rhyme this morning.

The dog and bone rang, so I went down the apples and pears to answer it. I sat on the stop and stare and wrote down the message with my Bill and Ben. Then I went out through the roof and floor with my finger and thumb.

Write what happened here.

Now make up your own rhyming code words here.

Writing tongue twisters

Try saying these tongue twisters. How fast can you say them?

She sells sea shells on the sea shore.

Peter Piper picked
a pickled pepper.

Cross Chris cracked
a cracking
Christmas cracker.

Parents

- This activity will teach your child how to write humour.
- Talk about words that are used to create humour and sound effects.

47

Now try to write your own tongue twisters.

Writing riddles

Match each riddle to
the correct object.

You can flick through me.
I am red with an a.
I am boo with a k.
What am I? ______

I run very fast.
I wear special shoes.
I eat sugar lumps and hay.
What am I? ______

I run very fast.
I wear special shoes.
I play in a team.
What am I? ______

I love dirty clothes.
I spin round and round.
Then I spit them out.
What am I? ______

football player

washing machine

book

horse

Parents

- This activity will teach your child how to write their own riddles.
- Help them to match the riddles to the objects, so they know how it's done.

47

Now write a riddle for these objects.

Writing a story

Who will be in your story?

____.

Who is the main character?

____.

What will happen?

____.

Where will it happen?

____.

How will it start?

____.

How will it end?

____.

Remember, illustrate means 'to draw' and border means 'the edge'.

- This activity will enable your child to write a sustained story.
- Offer guidance on the elements they need to remember – describing characters and places, setting, and rereading for sense.

Parents

47

Write your story here.

____

____

____

____

____

____

____

____

____

____

____

Now illustrate your story in the border of the page.

Writing information

Here is some information about a house that is for sale.

Address: 120, West View, Uptown, Shipperton.

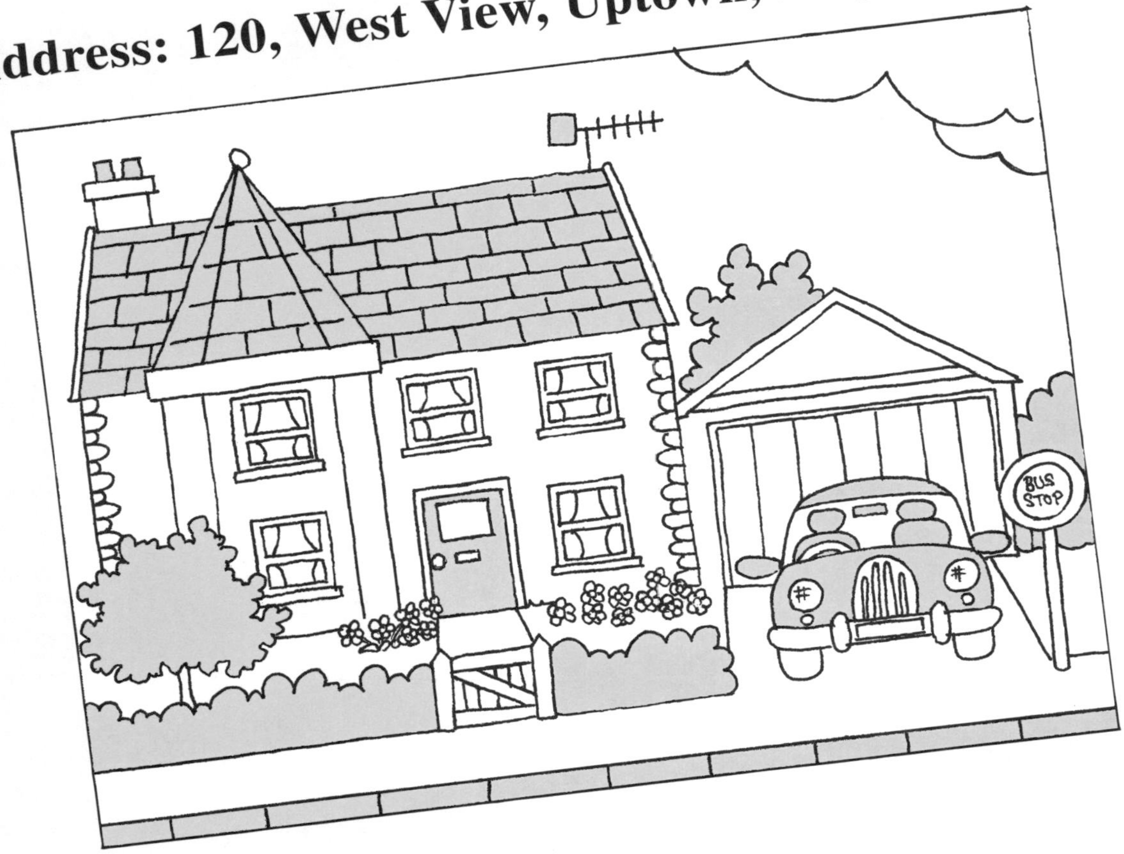

Rooms:	dining room kitchen two bathrooms sitting room three bedrooms
Outside:	back garden front garden garage for one car
Description:	The back garden is in the sun for most of the day. The house is close to good schools, and near a bus stop.

- This activity will help your child to present information and to use headings.
- Point out each heading before they start, and explain the term 'for sale'.

Parents 47

Draw a picture and write some information about your own home.

Address:

Rooms: ______________________________

____

____

____

____

Outside: ______________________________

____

Description: ______________________________

____

____

____

Further activities

4–5

Explain the difference between past and present. If something is happening now, it is present tense. If something has already happened, it is past tense. Make sure they match the verbs to pronouns correctly. For example, 'I am' and 'we are'.

Extend this further by asking them to change each sentence into the present tense. This will help them see how to use tenses in their own writing.

Answers: I jumped, I walked, We listened, I knocked, We laughed, I pushed. We are cooking, We are playing, I am watching, We are pulling, I am picking, We are planting.

6–7

Children are used to talking in different tenses, but find writing it much more difficult. So to help them, ask questions in the tense you want them to write in. If you ask in the past tense, your child will give an answer in the past tense, which they can then write down.

Ask your child to make a list of more past tense words that end in 'ed'. Then ask them to put each word into a short sentence, like 'I walked to the shops', or a longer one like 'I walked to school and played in the playground'.

Write lists of past and present tense words to help them learn the right spellings.

Answers: left, flew, ate, knocked, saw, chased, went.

8–9

Ask your child to write some instructions for a game you play at home, or to describe the way they get to school and home again. Ask them to draw a map and to write the instructions onto it, with arrows indicating which way to go.

Make sure the instructions are in the right sequence, and encourage them to number each one.

Instruction writing is impersonal, so make sure there is no use of 'I', 'we' or 'you'.

Answers: Instructions will vary.

10–11

Encourage your child to make up their own rhyming sentence. Then help them to write a few sentences that fit together.

Give them plenty of suggestions about how they could begin a sentence, 'I met...' 'I saw...' 'I had...' 'I spied...'. Then let them write their ideas independently.

Answers: log, van, house, coat, lizard, dish, road.

12–13

Extend this activity by asking your child to think of other words that have an opposite – boy/girl, man/woman, thick/thin, tall/small, nice/nasty. Then give them a sentence and ask them to write a sentence that has the opposite meaning.

Practise this further by looking at words which start with 'dis' or 'un', such as kind/unkind, happy/unhappy, satisfied/dissatisfied. You might like to tell your child a word with an opposite meaning to another word is called an antonym, but do not expect them to remember it yet.

Answers: pull, soft, rough, low, long, thin, small, slow, down, quiet.

1. This drink is freezing cold. 2. This jumper is very smooth. 3. That is low enough for me to reach. 4. My ruler is long enough to measure you.

4-15

- Practise compound words further by writing and drawing more – your child may already be familiar with the term 'compound'.
- Then write sentences first using a compound word, 'milkman' and then using each of the component words, 'man' and 'milk', so that your child sees how the words change their meaning.
- *Answers: milk man, pan cake, tea spoon, eye ball, snow man, butter fly, book shelf, gold fish = goldfish, sauce pan = saucepan.*

6-17

- Reinforce this activity by putting friends' names into alphabetical order. Then put family names into order, using the first letter of the first name if the surnames are the same.
- Put names into order that begin with the same letter, such as 'Sharon Clarke' and 'Amy Cook'. In this case, go to the second letter in the name to decide the order.

- *Answers: Charlie Adams, Christopher Baker, Abena Clarke, Parmi Dhak, Sam Evans, Amy Fisher, Laura Groves, Charlotte Hard, Kylie Irons, Roxanne Jackson, Michelle Knight, Nicholas Long.*

8-19

- Continue syllable work by asking your child to think of words with 4 syllables, then 5 syllables.
- How many syllables does their own name have?
- *Answers: dinosaur = 3 beats, children = 2 beats, dinner = 2 beats.*
  1 syllable – bed, two, what; 2 syllables – writing, going, sister, people, water, mummy;
  3 syllables – fantastic, elephant.

0-21

- Ask your child to think of other question words, foe example, 'How?' 'Do?' Ask them to write some questions to interview someone they know.

- Make sure they write a '?' at the end of each question.
- *Answers: Suggested questions might be – What is your name? Where do you live? When did you plant the beans? What did you do then? What are you going to do now?*

2-23

- With your child, look closely at which words rhyme and the number of syllables in each line, then ask them to write their own version.
- Extend this further by looking at another rhyme for example, *The Grand Old Duke of York*, in the same way, and asking your child to write their own version.

When children understand how rhymes are written, they will then be able to write their own.

- *Answers: The number of syllables in each line of both poems is 8, 6, 6, 6, and 7.*

Further activities

24-25

- The more experience children have at writing rhymes and poems, the better they will be able to write them independently.
- Develop this activity by giving your child different words to use in a rhyme, or a set of rhyming words to use such as 'stair' and 'stare', 'fair' and 'fare'. Then see if they can write down their own ideas, to then write their own poem.

If they need ideas to help them to get started, suggest a theme for them to write about, to example toys, or a monster comes to school.

26-27

- Extend this activity by searching through the stories for other character's phrases, and looking at other stories for well-known sayings.
- Ask your child to write a story and use a repetitive phrase of their own.
- *Answers: 1. Pinocchio, 2.The evil wolf, 3. Little Red Riding Hood, 4 Baby bear.*

28-29

- Practise story writing further by putting other well-known characters in different familiar settings, such as *Goldilocks and the Beanstalk* or *The Ugly Duckling meets Goldilocks*.
- See if your child can think of their own ideas, too. Make sure they uses a variety of ideas. Write some down together before they start writing their story.

30-31

- Read more fairy tales with your child and look for key words and phrases which describe each character.
- Ask your child to think of another character, draw it, and describe it in detail.
- Ask them to write a favourable profile, then an unfavourable one, about the same character.

32-33

- A word which has the same or similar meaning to another word is called a synonym.
- Introduce your child to a thesaurus. Look up a word in the thesaurus to find another word that means the same thing. 'How many words can you think of that you can use instead of *nice*?'
- *Answers: The synonyms will vary.*

4-35

- Ask your child to make up other rhyme codes, also known as rhyming slang. for example, 'What would rhyming slang for *dad* be?'.
- Extend this further by asking your child to write a story, substituting rhyming slang for real words.
- *Answer: The phone rang, so I went down the stairs to answer it. I sat on the chair and wrote down the message with my pen. Then I went out through the door with my mum.*

6-37

- When your child is writing their own tongue twister, make sure they mainly use words with the same first letter, words that nearly sound the same ('sells', 'shells'), and use some smaller words to fit it all together ('on', 'the', 'and').
- Help your child to write a tongue twister for every letter in the alphabet, or to write a sentence made up with words beginning with each letter of the alphabet. For example, 'A Big Cat Drew Every Flower Green, Hanging In Jars', and so on through the alphabet.

8-39

- To reinforce this activity, ask your child to write a riddle about an object at home, a person, or a place. Ask them to write a one sentence riddle – a very tricky game!
- *Answers: 1. book, 2. horse, 3. football player, 4. washing machine.*

0-41

- Make sure your child is able to use full stops and capital letters in all the right places. Teach them to put a full stop at the end of each idea, and to begin a new idea with a capital letter. Also remind them about capital letters on people's names.
- Develop the idea further by asking them to use speech marks when the characters speak. If they are not sure where to put speech marks, ask them to say the very first word a character says and the last word, and to put them there. You'll need to remind them several times before they use speech marks automatically.

2-43

- Look at some real information from estate agents. Focus on the headings they use, and how much information they give about a house.
- Explore this further by looking at passports, application forms, identity cards, and asking your child to write their own.

Celebration!

I can write a rhyme.

I can write some questions.

I can write a character profile.

I can write a story.